NOTRE DAME COLLEGE OF EDUCATION
MOUNT PLEASANT
LIVERPOOL L3 5SP

The Norwegians of Hemnesberget

ELIZABETH W. SAMUELS

KIM ELLIS

MARY C. DURKIN

TABA SOCIAL SCIENCE UNITS

ADDISON-WESLEY (CANADA) LIMITED
Don Mills, Ontario

TABA SOCIAL SCIENCE UNITS

Now Available
THE BEDOUIN OF THE NEGEV
THE THAI OF BANGKOK
THE NORWEGIANS OF HEMNESBERGET
THE PEOPLE OF OSAKA PREFECTURE

About the Authors

Elizabeth W. Samuels taught for many years in elementary schools in New Mexico and Massachusetts. Kim Ellis is a former teacher in the Richmond Unified School District, Contra Costa County, California, and was a member of the Taba Curriculum Project at San Francisco State College. Mary C. Durkin was associate director of the Taba Curriculum Project and a curriculum consultant for Contra Costa County.

A large group of social scientists and educators in Canada have been involved in the preparation of the Taba Social Science Units. Included in the group are: D. Ian Allen, assistant professor at the Professional Development Centre, Faculty of Education, Simon Fraser University, Burnaby, British Columbia; Phyllis R. Blakeley, assistant archivist in the Public Archives of Nova Scotia, Halifax; and Philip L. Wagner, professor of geography, Simon Fraser University, Burnaby, British Columbia.

ISBN 0-201-07484-2

TABA SOCIAL SCIENCE UNITS

General and Consulting Editors

Mary C. Durkin
Former Associate Director
Taba Curriculum Development Project
San Francisco State College

Anthony H. McNaughton
Professor of Education
University of Auckland
Auckland, New Zealand

Consultants for The Norwegians of Hemnesberget

John J. Gumperz
Professor of Anthropology
University of California, Berkeley

Robert A. LeVine
Professor, Human Resources and Anthropology
University of Chicago

Torleif H. Myhrer
Architect-Engineer
Lawrence Radiation Laboratory
University of California, Berkeley

Philip L. Wagner
Professor of Geography
Simon Fraser University
Burnaby, British Columbia

TO THE TEACHER

This unit, THE NORWEGIANS OF HEMNESBERGET, looks at the changes which have occurred in the small boat-building and fishing community of Hemnesberget in northern Norway. Grandfather Larsen can remember the early days when Hemnesberget was a market centre for the surrounding fishing and farming communities, when boats were still built in farm sheds during the long winter, and then dragged by sled to the small fjord town. Young Erik Larsen looks forward to an increasingly mechanized and less isolated future for his small community, and takes great delight in an unexpected visit to a Lapp village in the far north. The community is compared with that of the great ship-building city of Osaka in Japan when Erik's sister Britt tours the world on a Norwegian boat.

A Time of Dark

A cold, gray fog covered the hills and the town. The fog hid the distant mountain peaks from view. Snow was deep on the land.

It was noon, but the fog hid the sun. People came out of their houses and began walking down to the dock. They moved quickly to keep warm. Their steamy breath could be seen in the cold air.

A strong wind was coming across the water. If the wind kept blowing, the fog might lift. Then the sun would be seen low in the sky. Maybe the sun would shine for the launching of the new ship.

The water in Ranafjord does not freeze in winter. Boats can be launched at Hemnesberget at any time of year.

When a fishing boat is launched, few people come to watch. Many fishing boats are built in Hemnesberget. This new ship was larger and had a special purpose. Many people came to watch it slide down the ways into the water of the fjord.

The town of Hammerfest, in northern Norway, had ordered a 65-foot ship from the Larsen Boat Builders. The people who live in the district around Hammerfest would help pay for the ship. It was to be a medical ship. It would carry a doctor and a nurse, and many kinds of medicines. The ship would sail to farms and fishing villages on the fjords. There are no roads leading to these villages. The people live far from doctors and hospitals.

There are two boats in this picture. Can you see which is nearly ready to be launched? Can you see which boat has just been started?

Inside the boat shop, away from the wind, it was warmer and bright with lights. The special boat seemed to fill the large room. Erik Larsen and other boys and girls stood watching. Their fathers, their uncles, their big brothers were hard at work. They were the craftsmen who had built this ship.

The men had laid the keel, the backbone of the ship. Then they had shaped the ribs. The ribs and the keel were made of layers of wood, one on another, glued tight. This way of making keel and ribs is called laminating. It is not the old way. But laminated keel and ribs make a boat strong, so it will ride through the roughest seas.

These pictures show examples of laminating. In the model in the top picture, can you find the two ribs and the keel?

Planks are bent to fit the shape of the boat. Then they are bolted to the ribs. Can you find the ribs in these pictures?

The men had fitted planks to the ribs, bending them to the shape of the ship. The planks were held together with bolts and pegs. Now the ship was ready for the water, and the men were preparing to launch it.

There was another watcher, an older man with gray hair. Herr Larsen, Erik's grandfather, was watching his sons and his nephews. He was watching them get ready to launch the new ship.

Herr Larsen was no longer owner of the boat shop. His sons had taken over the shop, just as Herr Larsen had taken it over from his father. His sons were clever men. Herr Larsen watched them greasing the ways. The ship would slide down the ways into the water. They were using grease and green soap in the old way, these men who invented new tools to make better boats!

Herr Larsen looked over at young Erik. Erik would be a craftsman, too. He was quick to learn the use of a tool. But would the small shop be here when Erik grew to be a man? The old man wondered. Things were changing fast since the large boat factory had been built in Hemnesberget. Even now, Erik's older brother Nils had taken a job in the boat building factory. He had not come into the family shop.

In the large factory many boats are worked on at one time. The man has been using an electric sanding machine. Why do you suppose the boy is wearing a mask?

Can you find the ways where the boats slide into the water?

On each dock there is a hoist. What do you suppose it might be used for?

Now it was time! Most of the boys went outside to stand with the townspeople on the dock. Erik came to stand by his grandfather. The ways were ready, slippery with grease and soap. The men loosened the ship from the cradle that held it. They turned a jack to start the ship on its slide down the ways.

And now the silence. Voices hushed, hammers stilled. The new ship, the ship to carry help to the sick and hurt in lonely places, was making its way to the sea!

There was a great splash and a great cheer as the ship hit the water. It rolled a bit, back and forth, free now. Then smoothly it rode the water of the fjord. Men in a motorboat moved slowly up to take the line hanging from the bow of the ship. They towed it to the dock where it would stay until it was finished.

All the fine carpentry work was already done. The ship had wood panelling inside. There were cabins for sleeping, a dining room, a kitchen, and bathrooms. There was a special room for emergency operations. The machinery and the electrical connections had also been put in.

But there was still some work to be done while the ship floated at the dock. On the outside, the rigging had to be finished. The ship would have sails in case her engine failed. Machinery for lowering lifeboats must be installed. And, of course, all the medical equipment would have to be put in place.

This is the captain's cabin on a ship made in Hemnesberget. Behind the wheel is the compass. The circles in two of the windows keep the glass clear in snowy or icy weather.

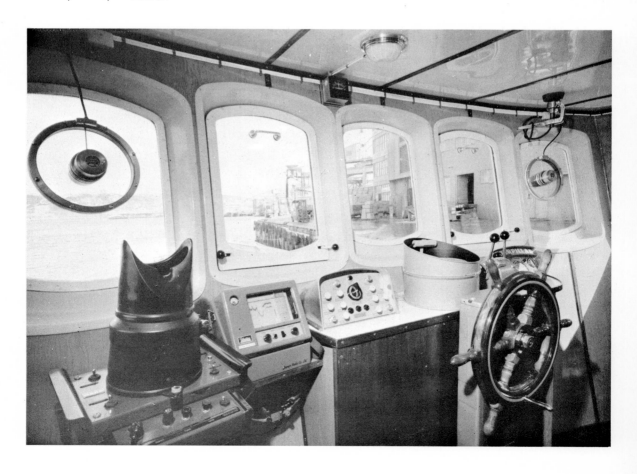

Hammerfest is one of the chief towns of northern Norway. Why did the people of this district need a medical ship?

A man had come from Hammerfest to see the launching of the ship. With him was a man from Oslo who worked for the Norwegian government. The doctor had come, too. He was there for the launching. He would also check the medical equipment as it went into the ship. He would stay on the ship when it sailed north.

Erik was right there with his father and grandfather when these people came up to shake hands. They shook hands with Erik, too. Then they all walked over the hard-packed snow to the Larsen house. Erik's mother and some of the other wives served hot coffee and cakes and cookies. There would be no more work in the shop today!

The Early Days

Some time later, Herr Larsen left the bright lights, the eating and drinking and talking. He walked back through the cold dark afternoon to the shop. There he found Erik. Erik was carving a little boat from a piece of wood.

Herr Larsen sat down on a bench. "Erik," he said, "let me tell you about the early days. A long time ago, we moved here to Hemnes from the farm. I was only a young boy."

Erik liked to listen to his grandfather. He often told stories of trolls, or of the old Norse gods, Thor and Odin and Loki. But now Grandfather was talking about real people, and about things that had really happened.

Why do you suppose Erik enjoys hearing about the early days of Hemnes?

In the early days women of Hemnes helped to pack fish in barrels. They earned extra money in this way.

"In those days, Erik, Hemnes wasn't much of a town. There were just boat sheds where fishermen could leave their boats in winter. And there was a church. The minister lived in a little village by the coast. About one Sunday a month he would come to the Hemnes church to hold a service.

"Hemnes was the centre. Farmers and fishermen would come to Hemnes from all around the fjord and the inland farms. They would come to hear the minister's sermon and to talk with each other. It was the only way they had, then, of sharing news with each other.

"Late fall was a time when many people came to Hemnes. The farmers, fishermen, and traders met in the town. The farmers brought handmade things of wood, leather, and wool. They also brought berries, cheese, and butter. The fishermen sold fish—fresh fish, dried fish, salted and smoked fish.

Stockfish are hung up to dry in northern Norway. What other methods of preserving fish are used?

"The traders brought in supplies like sugar and flour, coffee and tea. They also brought tools, and all the things a man might use for building. The farmers never had enough to sell to pay for what they bought. The traders gave them tools and supplies for the long winter. In the spring, the farmers would pay what they owed."

"How did they do that, Bestefar?" Erik asked his Grandfather. "There isn't any farming in the winter!"

"You are right, Erik!" Grandfather answered.

"Then how did the farmers earn money to pay the traders?" asked Erik again.

"In the winter, the farmers cut trees which they sold for lumber," said Grandfather. "They used some of the trees to make small fishing boats. In those days there were plenty of fish to be caught near the coast. Fishermen did not need to go in big boats far out to sea as they do now.

"The fir trees in our forests grow slowly and are full of small, hard knots. This is good strong wood for making boats. Farther north, tall trees of this kind do not grow. The farmers used their boats for fishing in the early spring. Then they sold them to the traders, and the traders sold them to fishermen in the north."

Herr Larsen watched Erik as he hollowed out the inside of the little boat. Erik was using a chisel. His grandfather looked at the big power tools in the shop.

What were the boats in this old picture used for? What do you notice about their size?

"In the early days, we didn't have the tools we have now. There was no electricity, either. My father had to find a bent tree to make the bow of a ship. Or he used a tree trunk and branch that had the right kind of curve. All through the long dark winter days, my father and his brothers would work on building a fishing boat. This was on the old farm, Erik, quite far from the fjord. In the spring, before the snow was melted, they hitched the horses to a large boat sled. The horses pulled the boat over the snow to the fjord to be sold to a trader."

Grandfather stood up and looked through the window. "One year, my father and his brother hauled the lumber instead, over the snow to Hemnes. They built a boat right here on this land, in their boat shed. That was the start. That was the beginning of the boat building business here. And it was the beginning of Hemnesberget as a town."

A horse-drawn sled was a common form of transportation in the early days.

This Viking ship is on display in a museum in Oslo, Norway. Can you see why a ship like this might not have been well suited for use far out at sea?

The Vikings

Herr Larsen stood looking out over the dark water of the fjord. The wind had died, and a light snow was falling. Everything was still. Then Erik spoke.

"Bestefar, was your father a Viking?"

"A Viking?" repeated Grandfather. He laughed. "No, the Vikings lived many long years before my father did. But why do you ask, Erik?"

"Our teacher, Laerer Olsen, told us there have always been boatbuilders around here. He showed us pictures of Viking ships. Laerer Olsen said that the Vikings sailed over almost the whole world in ships like those. He said the Vikings liked adventure and liked to fight."

19

Some of the old Viking farms are still in use after hundreds of years. What do you notice about the roofs of the buildings?

"That is true, Erik," answered Grandfather. "But Vikings did other things besides making trouble for people. They farmed and fished. They made salt from sea water and tar from the sap of the pine tree. They made tools, and they built very fine ships.

"There are farms west of Hemnesberget out on the coast. They were once the farms of Viking kings. I think that is where they built their ships. But they found the timber for their boats here near Hemnes.

"The Vikings made metal tools, but their ships were not put together with iron or copper rivets. They used strong leather straps to hold the boards together. They put tar in the joints to keep the water out. But the joints could move and give, so that the boats would hold together in rough seas."

Erik asked, "Bestefar, have you read about Leif Eiriksson? Laerer Olsen is reading to us about him in school. I think the Vikings must have been very brave and strong. They sailed all the way to America in those open ships!"

"Yes, I have read those stories, too. Leif Eiriksson may have been the very first man from Europe to land in America. The Norse men and women who settled there were brave and strong, too. They took cows and sheep in those ships all the way to America. They also built farms in the New World.

"No one knows how long the Vikings stayed in America, or really what happened to them. Perhaps there were too many Indians to fight. The Indians didn't like to have their land taken by strangers." Grandfather thought Erik would like to talk about the American Indians, but Erik was still thinking about the Vikings' ships.

This is a small part of a wall hanging made in France around the year 1100. It shows the kind of ships used by the Normans to conquer England. Many of the Normans were descended from Vikings. Can you tell where they got the design of their ships?

"I think I would like to be a sailor when I grow up, Bestefar," Erik said. "I would like to have adventures like the Vikings! I would like to see all the places Brit has seen!" Brit, Erik's older sister, works on a Norwegian ship.

"Well, Erik, you might," said Grandfather. "But I think one sailor in the family is enough. I hope you will stay in Hemnesberget like Nils and your father and your grandfather. I hope you will build ships as we have always done.

"Families in Hemnesberget like to stay together, Erik. Many of us could make more money in a city like Mo-i-Rana, in the steel factory. But it is better to be with the people you know, and to trade with families your father has traded with."

"Well, Bestefar, I like it here. Perhaps I will stay." Erik looked at the boat he had nearly finished. "I don't want to live in a city, ever! If I do sail away, I will always come home every year!"

How do you suppose these men would feel about the idea of moving away from Hemnesberget?

Do you think this picture of the aurora borealis was taken at night or during the day? How can you tell?

Winter Days

In winter the days become shorter and shorter. At Christmastime in the far north, the sun does not rise at all. People in Hemnesberget use electricity all day to light their homes, their shops, and their streets. Away from the town, over the hills and the fjords, sometimes there is only the light of the moon. Sometimes there is another kind of electric light in the sky. This is the aurora borealis, the "northern lights."

The aurora borealis fills the northern sky with colour: red, yellow, blue, green, and violet. The colours form many kinds of patterns in the sky. The light of the aurora borealis is not so bright as the moon.

These pictures show some of the ways of having fun in Hemnesberget during the winter. What are some of the ways that are not shown here?

When the moon is bright, the children like to play outdoors, even if it is very cold. In warm jackets, with mittens and caps and scarves and woolly socks, they ski and ice-skate. They build snow forts and have snowball fights. Sometimes they make snow huts and play inside by candlelight, or make slides on banks of deep, soft snow.

"Merry Christmas!"
in Hemnesberget.

At other times snow whirls swiftly out of the sky, or icy sleet soaks through woollen clothes. Then Erik and his friends must stay indoors. At home they read books and play games such as chess. Better than books or games, they like to use tools, to make things, to work in the shops. The boys and girls spend some wintry afternoons after school at the boat shops, the blacksmith's or the tinsmith's, the lumber mill or the electrical shop. At all of the shops, they watch and learn.

In the early days of building boats, trees from the forests around Hemnes were brought to the lumber mill in town. Here they were cut into planks. They were used for building boats and houses, docks, shops and stores.

Why do the carpenters of Hemnesberget like to buy lumber from the mill in their own town?

Now lumber comes from the whole district around Ranafjord. Some lumber is imported from places as far away as Africa, Asia, and America. It has been cut in standard sizes and shapes that boat builders, carpenters, and other woodworkers use.

The lumber mill in Hemnesberget was started by a group of Hemnes people many years ago. This group sold lumber to the boatbuilding families, or to the families of cabinetmakers. Now they still supply these shops with local wood and cut it to special sizes and shapes. They give special service to people they have worked with from early times. Large mills and factories do not give this kind of service.

The blacksmith's shop is one of Erik's favourite places. The fire in the forge flames high. The hammer rings as it strikes the red-hot, soft steel. Erik likes to hear the hiss and sizzle of the hot metal as it is plunged into the cold water.

In the early days, the blacksmith did more kinds of work than he does today. He made shoes for horses. He sharpened ploughs and other tools for farmers who now use tractors.

In the early days of boat building, the blacksmith made anchors and all the fittings for the ships. Some fittings are now bought from factories. But the blacksmith still makes many things for the ships. He uses copper, bronze, steel, and aluminum. He makes brackets and railings, special parts for anchors and hoists.

Erik and his grandfather visit the blacksmith's shop. Why do you suppose the blacksmith is called a craftsman?

For the children, the blacksmith makes steel hoops. They roll the hoops along in front of them with a stick. In payment, they run errands for the blacksmith.

The blacksmith's family has long served the people of Hemnesberget. They do not want the time to come when his work will not be needed. They want their children to be able to work and play in the forge. They want them to understand the skill of a good craftsman, and to know that before things can be bought, they must be made.

In the tinsmith's shop there are many kinds of machines and pieces of metal of all sizes and shapes. The tinsmith in the bottom picture is working on a ship's cabin. Why do you suppose the tinsmith is called a craftsman?

Why do you suppose children might enjoy helping to prepare middag?

Middag

Helga, Erik's mother, was happy. She sang to herself while she prepared middag, the midday meal. The kitchen was warm and steamy. Potatoes and carrots.were boiling on the stove. Meatballs and sauce were ready. Helga felt lucky she had meat in the freezer. Meat was more of a treat than fish, and today was a day for a treat.

Helga turned on the light in the dining room to set the table. She thought of the wonderful news she had to share with her family. If only Bestefar and Bestemor could be here to hear it too! Just then, through the window, she saw Erik coming up the hill on his skis. He had been practising for the boys' cross-country race.

Helga went quickly to the door to call Erik before he took off his skis.

How do you suppose Herr Larsen feels about going to his son's house for middag?

"Erik! Wait! Don't take off your skis yet! Will you please go to Bestemor's. Ask if they will come for middag. Say that I have a surprise. Say that I will telephone Nils to pick them up on his way home."

Erik turned his skis and headed off down the hill. Here was a chance to get some more practice. Every little bit helped to get his arms and legs strong. The cross-country race was several miles, and if his arms and legs were not strong, he would not last!

Erik crossed the field where the snow was soft and deep. It riffled over his skis and boots as each foot moved in easy rhythm.

"I wonder what Mor's surprise is?" Erik thought as he poled along. "She sounded excited." Soon he was at his grandparents' little house. They didn't live very far away.

By three o'clock, the Larsen family had gathered around the dining room table for middag. This is the big meal of the day. Father was home from the boat shop. Nils was home from the large boat factory. Erik was home from school. Bestefar and Bestemor were there, too. The only one who was away was Erik's big sister, Brit. She had been away for nearly a year.

Brit works on one of the big Norwegian ships that go to harbours around the world. Brit's ship carries rice from Thailand to Japan, and manufactured goods from Japan to Thailand. Brit sent a kite to Erik the first time she was in Bangkok. She sent Christmas presents to everyone in the family from Japan. But Erik really was not thinking about Brit at all.

Norway's fleet of cargo ships is one of the largest in the world.

How do you suppose the Larsens feel about having guests for middag?

Erik listened to the talk going around the table. Father was telling Bestemor about the new book he was reading. Nils and Bestefar were talking about the ski jumping contest they had seen on television. The men who won were going to represent Norway in the Olympic Games. Erik was sure Nils was a good enough ski jumper to be in the Olympics. Mor thought so, too, and she often told Nils to try out. But today Helga was not saying much. She just made sure everyone had plenty of butter for their bread, and smiled happily over her secret.

Finally middag was finished and the dishes cleared away. The Larsens sat in the living room around the fireplace.

"Well, Helga," said Far. "Tell us what makes you feel so happy."

"Yes! Yes, Karl. Today I had a letter from Brit. A special letter. I wanted to read it to all of you together." Mor slipped the letter from the pocket of her skirt, opened it and began to read.

The Letter

Dear Mor,

Thank you for your good letter and all the news from home. I laughed at your story of how Far won the fishing contest. I liked the picture you sent of him sitting by the hole in the ice, pulling out the fish.

Yesterday I went to the Norwegian Seamen's Church here in Osaka. As you know, the Norwegian Seamen's Churches are owned by the Norwegian Seamen's Mission. The service is just the same as in the church at home. In faraway places the church does many different kinds of things for us. Providing church services is just one part of what they do.

Erik and his cousins fish through the ice.

The church finds interesting things for us to do while we are in port. The church took a group of Norwegians to the Osaka shipbuilding harbour. I, of course, went with them. The Japanese are great shipbuilders. They are building some of Norway's largest cargo ships.

I wished Far and Bestefar had been there with me. They would have looked at everything and asked many more questions than I did!

These factories are much bigger and much busier than the shops where I used to play. There is no room for children in the Osaka shipyards!

I know our boatbuilding business will have to grow. But I hope it never gets so big as this! Even Mo-i-Rana is a lot more quiet than Osaka!

In what ways do you suppose shipbuilding in Osaka is different from shipbuilding in Hemnesberget? In what ways might it be similar?

And now, I have a surprise! Next month I am coming HOME! I will take a jet plane from Don Muang Airport in Bangkok on the fifth. I will be in Hemnesberget on the seventh. I send you my flight plan home.

LEAVE		ARRIVE		FLYING TIME
Bangkok	9:30 a.m.	London	7:20 a.m.	5 hours
London	11:25 a.m.	Oslo	2:15 p.m.	2 hours
Oslo	7:50 p.m.	Bodö	9:15 p.m.	1½ hours

From Bodö I will take the early train. It gets into Finneidfjord at 1:25 p.m.

Erik can find the cities on the globe. He may think the flying time between Bangkok and London is a puzzle! Can he find the answer?

How many hours of difference is there between Bangkok time and London time? How many hours between London time and Oslo time? How does this help to explain Brit's flight plan?

PLACE	BANGKOK	LONDON	OSLO
TIME	9:30 A.M.	2:30 A.M.	3:30 A.M.

How exciting it is! I think about skiing in the spring with all of you! We will climb Hemnes Mountain and ski down to that wonderful sunny spot for lunch. We will pack the old coffeepot full of snow and hang it over the fire, then let the coffee boil for just a minute or two. I can almost smell it now! What fun!

And thinking of smells, I will have again the good smell of the birch trees coming into new leaf! And I will see again the bright spring flowers pushing up through the snow! I can hardly wait to get home.

Spring skiers pass a horse-drawn sled. Are these forms of transportation old or new in Hemnesberget?

How do you suppose the Larsens and their guests feel about Brit's letter?

How long I will be in Hemnesberget, I do not know. I am sure to be there until after Sankt Hans. Later I will go to the Norwegian Seamen's School in Oslo.

I want to have a better job than the one I have now, serving the officers their food. At school I will learn to be a communications engineer. I will get better pay, a longer vacation, and more freedom on the ship.

Please give my love to Bestemor and Bestefar. Tell them I will write to them in the next few days.

With love to all,
Brit

Mother finished reading. Erik, jumping up and down, began to shout, "Brit is coming home! Brit is coming home!" He ran over and hugged Grandfather. "You see, Bestefar! Even Brit is coming home!"

Grandfather laughed, "Yes, Erik, even Brit comes home. Still, I wish she would stay in Hemnesberget. I don't see how she can be happy so far from her own people."

"She is living with Norwegians on the ship," said Nils. "At home, in a way, and yet seeing the world. Not a bad life!"

"That is true, but they are not Norwegians from Hemnesberget," Mor put in. "She might as well be in Mo-i-Rana."

"Oh, Helga, if Brit were in Mo she would come home every weekend," Far said. "We all wish she would live in Hemnesberget with us. Most of our relatives do. But Brit was always restless. She always liked to wander, to hike in the woods, and to climb mountains."

Spring in Hemnesberget means bright flowers as well as snow.

How is springtime fun in Osaka different from springtime fun in Hemnesberget?

Erik was studying the globe. "Look, Far. Why doesn't Brit fly home from Osaka? It is closer that way."

Far went over to look at the globe with Erik. "I think she must stay with the ship for one year, Erik. That year will be finished next month. By then the ship will be back in Bangkok. When Brit gets to Finneidfjord, you and Bestefar and I will be there to meet her."

Grandmother, knitting quietly by the fire, was remembering when she was as young as Brit. All girls in those days stayed home.

"I believe Brit is happy," Grandmother thought. "I believe I would have liked being a sailor, too." Grandmother laughed to herself at the thought.

A Time of Light

It was Saturday, the first day of the ski meet. The weather was cold and crisp, the snow dry and fast. Sunshine broke through the scattery clouds.

Most of the townspeople came to watch the races. For many years, an old farm had been the starting place for cross-country races and relay races.

The Boys' Cross-country was the first race of the day. The boys formed a line at the starting place. They would start half a minute apart, and all would ski the same course.

Nils and Far watched Erik start. For much of the race Erik was out of sight. Nils and Far waited patiently for him to reappear. Finally Erik came toward the finish. He had made good time.

When they were not racing, the boys climbed to the tops of the bare birch trees to watch the grown-ups' cross-country runs. They played like monkeys in the treetops much of the time. It is hard to sit still, even watching the most important ski races of the year. Cross-country races take time.

The start of a cross-country race many years ago. What do you see in the trees?

Why do you suppose the people of northern Norway have always been good cross-country skiers?

Cross-country skiers need to be strong and fast. They must be able to climb steadily up the hills. They must be able to ski swiftly downhill, over difficult trails. They must not get tired pushing along for many miles. Cross-country racers are judged on how fast they can ski over the course.

Sunday was ski jumping day. Everyone was out early. The hill on each side of the ski jump was covered with people. People came from Korgen and Finneidfjord, and some even from Mo, to watch the jumping. People in Norway never tire of seeing a ski jumper sail high over the treetops. A lone figure against the sky, his arms at his side, his body almost lying straight along his skis, the ski jumper soars to a landing far below.

Each skier makes three jumps. Judges give the skier points for each jump. They give points for how far the skier jumps. They give points for the way he sails through the air, and for the way he lands on the hill below. A skier probably makes a different number of points each time he jumps. All points for each jumper are added together by the judges. The ski jumper with the most points wins. There is a special prize for the most beautiful jump of the day.

On Sunday night the winners were announced and prizes were given out. The lights of the school gym shone on the silver and gold cups.

There are ski jumping contests until late in the spring. How can you tell this is a warm day?

The finish line! How do you think Eric felt about winning the race?

The officers of the sports club and the judges of the ski meet took their places on the platform. The sounds of laughter and chatter were hushed. It was time for the names of the winners of each race and each jumping contest to be called.

"Erik Larsen! First place, Boys' Cross-country, three-mile race!" read the secretary of the sports club.

Erik turned beet-red. Nils gave him a little push, and Erik was climbing the steps to the platform. There in front of him stood the president of the sports club. In his hand was a splendid silver cup.

Then, all at once, the cup was in Erik's hand. He was shaking hands with the president and thanking him. Erik's smile reached from ear to ear as he walked back to Nils and Mor and Far.

How do you suppose the people living on Ranafjord travelled to Bodö before the roads and railroads were built?

Going to the Station

Karl Larsen drove carefully along the road. Patches of melting snow made the going slippery. Snow no longer covered the rolling meadows beside the road. Sparkling bright spring flowers of blue, white, and yellow were blooming. Pink and yellow buds were pushing through snow not yet melted by the warm sun. The light green leaves of the birch trees showed clearly against the blue sky. It was just the kind of a day Brit had been looking forward to.

And now Brit was on the train, on her way to Finneidfjord. Erik, Bestefar, and Far would be at the station when the train came in. Erik wanted to tell Far to hurry, hurry, hurry! Far and Bestefar were so busy talking, Erik thought they must have forgotten all about Brit!

Far was saying, "I went to the meeting of the City Council last night. I listened to your report on the new ferry."

"Yes, Karl. I was proud to give that report! Think how much good is coming out of the work we did these past few years."

Erik suddenly was interested. "You mean the new ferry, Bestefar? The one that meets the road to the coast? Did you start that ferry, Bestefar?"

How does the ferry help the people of Hemnesberget?

"No, Erik, I didn't start the new ferry service. The Larsen Boat Shop didn't even build the ferryboat. But as a member of the City Council, I helped our city to get the ferry and to keep it going. All of the Council members worked together to bring the ferry to Ranafjord."

Erik said, "Our teacher, Laerer Olsen, said that he can take us to see the old Viking farms on the coast. He says the new ferry and the new road have made it easy to go to the coast now."

Grandfather laughed. "I wish I had known Laerer Olsen's plans. I would have put 'Trips by School Children' into my report, too."

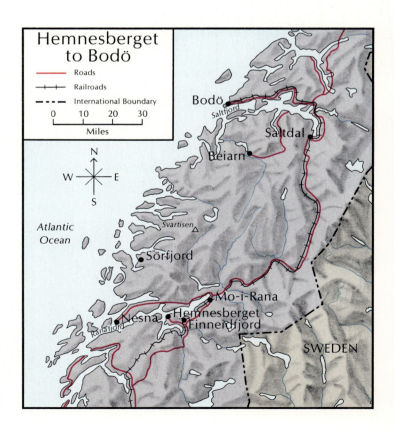

What directions did Brit travel from Bodö to Finneidfjord? How far did she travel? How far is it from Hemnesberget to Finneidfjord?

What forms of transportation can you find in this old picture of Hemnesberget?

"The new ferry helps in many ways, Erik," said Far. "More people come to Hemnesberget from the coast now. They buy things in our town, even if they are going on to Mo-i-Rana. This helps all of us."

"My friend Petter says that his whole family took the new ferry to go on a picnic last Sunday. I guess there are lots of good things about the ferry," Erik said.

Far turned into the station and parked the car. Erik was more sure than ever that Bestefar knew everything and could do anything. But there was Brit, waving to them from the train! Erik began to run. He threw himself into Brit's arms.

Sankt Hans

It was June. Erik and his friends rowed and swam in the fjord. They hiked on trails across the hills and rode bicycles through the town. They hoped the good weather would last till past Sankt Hans—Midsummer Night.

The boys had roamed over the shores of the fjord collecting piles of driftwood. They had walked through the woods picking up fallen branches. They were getting ready for Midsummer Night, when the light of the sun never leaves the hills around Hemnes.

Erik and his friends have only a short time each year to ride their bicycles. Why do you suppose this is true?

This picture was taken on Midsummer Night. What do you notice about the sky?

Sankt Hans! The Eve of St. John, Midsummer Night! Just what the best part of Sankt Hans was, Erik wasn't sure. He had always been so sleepy he could not stay awake for the big fire at midnight. Last year Mor had tried and tried to waken him when the bonfires were burning their brightest. This year, it would be different! This year he would stay awake!

Now Far and Bestefar waited in the Larsen boat for the rest of the family. They were all going across the fjord to the summer cabin for Sankt Hans. The driftwood collected by the boys was already packed in the boat. There was also scrap wood from the boat shop, left over from the fishing boat now being built.

Mor and Bestemor and Brit had packed baskets of food. There were sandwiches and cakes and cookies. There was coffee and lemonade. There was a special treat, "egge dosis." Erik had watched his mother whip eggs and sugar together to make the frothy, creamy dessert.

Ever since the early days there have been bonfires on Midsummer Night. Sometimes there are contests to see who can build the biggest fire. Why do you suppose Norwegian people like to spend a lot of time outdoors during the summer?

The other Larsen families were already on their way across the fjord. Some of them had been at the cabin all day. They had brought food and firewood, and they had collected a great pile of seaweed. Helga's father and mother and her brother Ole had come in from the family farm. There would be aunts and uncles and cousins from both sides of the family.

At midnight, all around the fjord, there would be bonfires. There had been bonfires burning on Midsummer Night around these shores for hundreds of years. Families and friends, young and old, met together for picnics and fun. The fires were piled high with wood to make the biggest possible blaze. Seaweed, or sometimes coal tar, was put on the fires to make a heavy, black smoke. There was no dark of night to show the brightness of the flames, so dark black smoke would do instead.

After supper, all the young people gathered around Bestefar and Bestemor. Bestefar began to tell some of the tales of long ago. First he told stories about Midsummer Night in other places. There are many beliefs about bonfires. In some countries, people thought fires built on roads and open spaces would keep sickness away from cattle. Other people built fires to keep witches away.

Bestefar told how at one time in Norway fires were lit at places where two roads met. Nine kinds of wood were burned and everyone threw toadstools into the fire. This was supposed to stop the power of trolls and other evil spirits. The children wanted to hear more about trolls, so Bestefar told them about the boy who had an eating contest with a troll.

On Sankt Hans Eve bonfires on shore can be seen from passing ships.

Ash Lad and the Troll

Once there was an old farmer who had three lazy sons. The farmer owed more money than he could pay. He himself was too old and sick to do much work, and his sons never lifted a finger. The youngest son was known as Ash Lad. He sat by the fire and poked in the ashes all day long. The older boys were not much better.

A good forest was part of the farm. The old farmer could sell wood to pay his debts if his sons would chop the trees. At last the boys agreed.

Early in the morning the eldest son started off with a big axe over his shoulder. When he came to the forest he began to chop a scraggly fir tree. He had not hit many blows when a huge troll came through the trees.

"If you chop wood in my forest, I will kill you!" the troll said in a terrible voice.

In fear for his life, the boy threw down the axe and ran for home. When his father, the old farmer, heard what had happened he said, "You are a chicken-hearted silly! No troll ever scared me when I was young!" But his son would not go back to the forest.

The next morning the second son went off with a big axe over his shoulder. No troll would scare him! He came to the forest and began to chop a scraggly fir tree. He had not hit many blows when the huge troll came through the trees.

"If you chop wood in my forest, I will kill you!" The troll's voice was really terrible!

In fear for his life, the boy threw down the axe and ran for home. The old farmer was angry when he heard what had happened.

"You are as silly as your brother! No troll ever scared me when I was young!" But his son would not go back to the forest.

The next morning Ash Lad was getting ready to go to the forest.

"You!" his brothers yelled. "You are going to the forest? You have never been out of the house! Do you think you can outwit the troll?"

Ash Lad didn't say much about that, but he asked for a big lunch. His mother gave him some bread and cheese to put in his knapsack. Off Ash Lad went with a big axe over his shoulder. When he came to the forest he began to chop a scraggly fir tree. Very soon the troll came through the trees.

"If you chop wood in my forest, I will kill you!" the troll bellowed. Ash Lad took the cheese out of his knapsack.

"Hold your tongue!" he shouted to the troll. "Or shall I squeeze you the way I squeeze water out of this stone?"

The troll saw water trickle from Ash Lad's clenched fist. He said, "No, no! Don't do that, dear boy! I'll help you to chop the wood!"

The troll was good at chopping, and they soon cut up plenty of wood. Then the troll said, "Come to my house for supper. Your house is far, but my home is near."

So Ash Lad and the troll went off together through the woods. When they came to the troll's cave, the troll said, "Take these buckets to the well for water. I will build the fires."

Ash Lad saw at once that he could not even lift the big iron pots from the floor.

"I won't bother with these little thimbles," said Ash Lad. "I will bring back the whole well, instead."

"No, no! Don't do that, dear boy!" said the troll. "I need my well. I will bring the water, and you build the fires."

When this was done the troll cooked a huge pot of porridge. When they sat down to eat, Ash Lad said, "If you are willing, let's have an eating contest." The troll was sure he could win at this game, so he agreed.

The troll was so busy pushing porridge into his mouth that he did not watch Ash Lad. The boy tied his knapsack under his chin and scooped porridge into that. When the knapsack was full, Ash Lad took his knife and ripped a hole in it. Then he went on scooping. The troll saw Ash Lad cut the hole with his knife, but he just kept on eating. But at last the troll put down his spoon.

"I can't eat another bite!" said the troll.

"You must eat!" said Ash Lad. "I'm not half full. Do what I did. Cut a hole in your stomach. Then you can eat as much as you want."

"Doesn't that hurt?" asked the troll.

"Oh, nothing to worry about," answered Ash Lad.

So the troll cut a hole in his stomach, and that was the end of him! Ash Lad found the silver and gold the troll had hidden in his cave. Ash Lad took it all home. He paid off the old farmer's debts, and had some left over.

A Camping Trip

One day near the end of July, Erik was on his way to Ostrand's Sporting Goods store to look at fishing poles. Far had been talking with Nils about going fishing in the mountain streams. Erik hoped Far might take him along, too. He wanted to be prepared.

In front of the Co-operative Store Erik met his friend Mattis, the Lapp boy. Lapps are another people living in northern Norway. They live not only in Norway, but in Sweden and Finland, too. In the mountains around Hemnes, Laplanders have large herds of reindeer from which they get their living. They drive the herds from the mountains to the coast in spring. They move back to the mountains in fall.

A Lapp family shops in a small store. What kinds of things will they buy?

The Lapp family who lives in this tent has gone to town to sell reindeer skins. They have shut their tent so passers-by will know they are not home.

Some of the Lapp families who live close to Hemnes have houses to live in, not just tents. Mattis, Erik's friend, was in Erik's grade at school.

"Hello, Erik!" said Mattis.

"Goddag, Mattis. What are you doing in town? I thought you had followed the reindeer north."

"Yes, we are camped up in the mountains north of Hemnes," answered Mattis. "But Father sent my brother Jo and me to town. My mother needs more coffee and sugar. My father wants more tobacco."

"Where is Jo? I didn't see him," Erik said.

"Jo has gone to find some of his friends. Father says we may bring some of them back to camp with us. Would you like to come?"

Erik stared at Mattis. Would he like to come? Would he like to visit the Lapp camp? To follow the reindeer! He must be dreaming!

"Well!" said Mattis. "Have you lost your voice? Don't you want to come? We will go toward Svartisen, the Black Glacier. We will camp out and fish in the streams. Perhaps I will teach you to lasso the deer."

"Oh, Mattis!" Erik let out his breath. "Of course I will come! That is, I will come if Mor will let me. I'm sure she will! Far will tell her I am big enough. She will see that you came alone to town with Jo. Come home with me now and we shall talk to Mor!"

Mor listened carefully to what the boys had to say. She did not see the grown-up boy that Erik felt himself to be. Had she forgotten that Erik had won the three-mile cross-country race?

To separate a reindeer from the rest of the herd, a Lapp boy swings his lasso over the antlers and neck. Then the animal is pulled out of the corral. He will be trained to pull sleds.

With a lasso at the ready over his shoulder, a Lapp herdsman keeps watch over his herd. What do you think might happen to the herd if they were not watched?

"No, Erik. I have not forgotten. But three miles on skis is not the same as ten or more miles on foot! But let us go over to the boat shop and talk to Far."

Far listened carefully to the boys. Then he listened carefully to what Mor had to say.

"Well, Helga, I do agree that Erik's legs are still pretty short," Far said, looking at his son. "Still, Erik's legs are sturdy, and he is not a baby any more. Mattis, what does Jo say if you fall behind on the trail?"

"Jo is easier on other boys than he is on me, Herr Larsen," Mattis said with a laugh. "He will look after Erik. Our father told him I could bring Erik, and Jo is really kind."

"What do you say, Helga? Shall Erik follow the reindeer?"

"It is a wonderful trip for him to take. Erik must go," said Mor at last. "He will sleep very well after such a long hike. Erik, you will need to get your things together. You need your sleeping bag and some heavy clothes. It will be cold as you go toward Svartisen."

"Far, I want to buy a fishing pole!" cried Erik. "And a knife! May I have a knife like Mattis's to wear in my belt?"

"Right, Erik! Go to Herr Ostrand's Sporting Goods store and tell him what you need. Make a list. And ask Herr Ostrand for the new mosquito oil. The mosquitoes are hungry up toward Svartisen. Long ago the Laplanders used birch bark oil. But this new oil is better, and it doesn't dye your skin."

This Lapp mother lights the fire in the middle of the floor to heat water for coffee. What things do you see that you might see in other homes in Hemnesberget?

61

Erik began writing out a list of things to take.

sleeping bag	*bread*
fishing pole	*flatbröd*
knife	*fenaknok (smoked*
boots	*dried meat)*
sweaters	*mosquito oil*

"Helga," said Far, "when the boys are all ready to go, you and Brit can take them across the fjord. They can spend the night at the old farm. That will give them an early start up the mountain to the Lapp camp."

The Lapp at the right is starting to skin a reindeer. His wife is busy hanging up the carcass on a special stand.

People come from all over Ranafjord to test their boats and their skill as sailors.

Boat Races

Summer is a short season in Hemnesberget. By the end of July the wind and rain can be icy cold. People begin to think about fall and winter. Soon Brit would leave for school in Oslo. It would soon be time for Erik's school to begin. But today was warm and sunny, and everyone was thinking about other things.

Herr Larsen stood with his son Karl and his grandson Erik on the deck of a new fishing boat. Herr Larsen thought it was one of the best boats the Larsens had ever built. Karl would race it tomorrow on the second day of the boat races. He would race it against other fishing boats. Older fishing boats as well as new ones and boats from other places would be in the race. Herr Larsen was sure that the changes in design would help this boat to win easily!

This old picture shows a Nordlands rowboat in the background. In what way is the boat like a Viking ship?

Today there would be races for other kinds of boats. There would be motorboat races for wooden boats and for fibreglass boats. There would be races for speedboats and rowboats.

The three Larsens were waiting for the rowboat races to begin.

Many people had gathered to watch the Nordlands rowboat race. These boats are made to glide through the water as swiftly and easily as the old Viking ships. The rowboats are smaller, but their shape is like the shape of the Viking ships. The rowboats have a high bow and high stern. The bow has a crosspiece on it which is copied from the old Viking ships.

Nils was rowing with three of his cousins. Erik watched until they disappeared behind an island. Then he spoke.

"Bestefar? Nils says a circus used to come for the boat race weekend. Why doesn't it come here any more?"

"Long after people left their farms and came to live by the fjord," Bestefar answered, "they had a Trade Fair at the end of the summer. As farming became less important, the Fair changed. Instead of butter and cheese and lumber and fish, people began to sell things they made. Men sold boats. Women sold handwoven scarves and knitted socks and mittens.

This picture was taken in Hemnesberget many years ago. How can you tell a celebration is going on?

"The Fair was always a time for fun. People came from many different places. Sometimes a circus came to town. Now we don't have a Fair any more, but people still come from far away to see the boat races. I believe there will always be boat races here for as long as Hemnesberget is a boat-building town."

Bestefar finished talking. He looked out over the water. All the boats he could see were quite different from the boats his father used to make. Little by little the patterns had changed with the need for different kinds of boats. Little by little the tools had changed, and the ways of working.

What can you find in this old picture of Hemnesberget that has not changed very much?

What things can you find in this picture of Hemnesberget that were probably not there many years ago?

What differences can you find between this old picture of Hemnesberget and the new picture below?

What things can you find in this picture that might change if Hemnesberget continues to change?

Bestefar remembered how his father had decided to leave the farm. His father knew he could make a good living by building boats. He did not really need to farm. He saw that it would be easier to pull the lumber to the fjord than to pull a finished boat. He saw that it would be easier to build boats in the boatshed by the water than way up on the farm.

Herr Larsen sees that still greater changes will come to Hemnes in the future. He wants Erik to know how the boat building business and the town grew up together. Bestefar thinks Erik will make good use of the present if he knows how things were in the past.

Scandinavia

- - - International Boundaries

⊛ National Capitals

0   100   200
Miles

Hammerfest

Tromsö

Murmansk

Narvik

Bodö

Hemnesberget

Atlantic Ocean

FINLAND

Kaunas

Trondheim

NORWAY

SWEDEN

Tampere

Turku

Leningrad

Helsinki

Bergen

Oslo

Tallinn

Stockholm

Göteborg

Riga

U.S.S.R.

North
Sea

Århus

DENMARK

Copenhagen
Malmö

Baltic   Sea

N

Vilnius

W   E

Gdynia
Danzig

Kaliningrad

GERMANY   POLAND

S

What city is the capital of Norway? What
direction would you travel to get from the capital
to Hemnesberget? How far would you have to
travel?

The Midnight Sun

The earth rotates, or spins around, once every 24 hours. The rotation of the earth causes day and night. On the part of the earth facing toward the sun, it is daytime.

The earth also revolves, or travels around the sun, once each year. The revolution of the earth causes differences in number of hours of daylight. As you can see on the diagram, the earth is tilted. There are more hours of daylight on the part of the earth tilted toward the sun.

The northern part of the earth has more hours of daylight between March 21 and September 22. In northern Norway, for a few days during the winter, the sun does not appear at all. For a few days during the summer, the sun shines even at midnight.

The Lapps

The Lapps live in the mountains of northern Norway, Sweden, and Finland. Reindeer are very important to the Laplanders. They provide the Lapps with food and clothing. The reindeer also pull sleds and carry large packs on their backs.

(Above) Lapps must drive their herds across water as well as land. The lead reindeer has a bell tied around his neck, and the sound of the bell causes the rest of the herd to follow him into the water. The boats must be kept as close as possible to the swimming herd to keep the reindeer from swimming off in all directions. If the smaller animals have trouble swimming across, they may need to be lifted into the boat.

(Left, page 71) Some Lapps live in houses close to villages, and may even drive cars. Lapps arrive at church for a wedding on foot and by car.

(*Top right*) A Lapp bride and groom return to the groom's home to celebrate their marriage. The celebration will last several days, and the best reindeer meat will be served to the guests.

(*Bottom right*) Lapps who live in or near villages send their children to Laplander Schools. There they are taught their own language and the Lapp way of life. The girl is learning how to make Lapp clothing.

The Lapps make much use of reindeer skins. They use them for blankets and rugs. They make clothing out of them. They sell them to Norwegians and tourists. Before the skins can be used, they must be treated and dried.

(Left) A Lapp woman is working on a reindeer skin.

(Top right) Reindeer skins hang out to dry on the walls of a shed.

Many Lapps travel with their herds seeking good pasture. They live in tents, and may be on the move for weeks at a time. The Lapps shown on this page and on page 71 are called "fixed-dwelling" Lapps. They live in houses, and may even farm and raise cows rather than reindeer.

(Bottom right) These girls are stacking hay which will be fed to cattle.

Thinking About the Norwegians

1. Pretend that you are a friend of Erik. You live in Hemnesberget and go to the same school as Erik. You enjoy the same activities as Erik and his friends.

Make a list of the things you like to do in the Time of Dark. Make a list of the things you like to do in the Time of Light. The pictures on this page may give you some ideas. Choose one thing from these two lists that you think is the best thing about living in Hemnesberget. Then find a way to tell about it.

You might use a drawing or several drawings. A sentence, a rhyme, or a riddle might be your way to tell about Hemnesberget.

2. Look back through all the pictures of Hemnesberget. Choose a picture that you think shows the most important thing about Hemnesberget. Find someone in your class who has chosen the same picture. Find out whether he chose it for the same reason you did. Report to the class which picture you and your partner chose, and why.

Glossary

This glossary contains some of the foreign words and names in this book. You can use the glossary as you would use a dictionary. The glossary will give you the meanings of the foreign words, and will show you how to pronounce the foreign words and names.

The pronunciation of each word is shown just after the word, in this way: **ab bre vi ate** (ə brē′vē āt). The letters and signs used are pronounced as in the words below. The mark ′ is placed after a syllable with primary or heavy accent, as in the example above. The mark ′ after a syllable shows a secondary or lighter accent, as in **ab bre vi a tion** (ə brē′vē ā′shən). (From *Thorndike-Barnhart Beginning Dictionary* by E. L. Thorndike and Clarence L. Barnhart. Copyright © 1968 by Scott, Foresman and Company. Reprinted by permission.)

a	hat, cap	f	fat, if	o	hot, rock	u	cup, butter	ə	represents:
ā	age, face	g	go, bag	ō	open, go	u̇	full, put		a in about
ã	care, air	h	he, how	ô	order, all	ü	rule, move		e in taken
ä	father, far			oi	oil, voice	ū	use, music		i in April
		i	it, pin	ou	house, out				o in lemon
		ī	ice, five			v	very, save		u in circus
b	bad, rob			p	paper, cup	w	will, woman		
ch	child, much	j	jam, enjoy	r	run, try	y	young, yet		
d	did, red	k	kind, seek	s	say, yes	z	zero, breeze		
		l	land, coal	sh	she, rush	zh	measure, seizure		
e	let, best	m	me, am	t	tell, it				
ē	equal, be	n	no, in	th	thin, both				
ėr	term, learn	ng	long, bring	ᵺH	then, smooth				

The Norwegians of Hemnesberget

Bestefar (best′ə fär)
Bestemor (best′ə mür)
Bodö (bü′du̇)
Brit (brit)
egge dosis (egə dü′sis) — *a Norwegian dessert*
Erik (i rik)
Far (fär) — *father*
fenaknok (fen′ə knôk) — *smoked dried meat*
Finneidfjord (fin′nā fyürd)
fjord (fyürd) — *narrow inlet of the sea*
flatbröd (flät′brüd) — *a thin wafer of bread*
goddag (gô däg′) — *good day*
Hemnesberget (hem′nes berg′et)
Helga (hel′gə)
Jo (yü)
Karl (kärl)
Korgen (kür′gen)
Laerer Olsen (lar′ər ül′sen)
Leif Eiriksson (lāf ā′rik sôn)

Loki (lü′kē) — *old Norwegian god*
Mattis (mā tēs′)
middag (mid′däg) — *midday meal*
Mo-i-Rana (mü′ ē rä′nä)
Mor (mür) — *mother*
Nils (nils)
Nordlands (nürd′länds)
Odin (ü′din) — *old Norwegian god*
Ole (ü′le)
Oslo (ôs′lü) — *capital of Norway*
Ostrand (ô′stränd)
Petter (pet′er)
Ranafjord (rä′nə fyürd) — *fjord Hemnes is located on*
Sankt Hans (sänkt häns′) — *Eve of St. John, Midsummer Night*
Svartisen (svärt′i sen) — *mountain north of Hemnes*
Thor (tür) — *old Norwegian god*
troll (trül) — *a giant of Norwegian folklore who lived in a cave*

Photograph Acknowledgments

Cover and page 4	Valerie Stalder
6-10	Torleif Myhrer
11	John Gumperz
12	Torleif Myhrer
14	Valerie Stalder
15	Torleif Myhrer
16	Doris H. Linder
17	Torleif Myhrer
18	Torleif Myhrer
20	John Gumperz
21	Erich Lessing, Magnum
22	Torleif Myhrer
23-25	Valerie Stalder
26	Torleif Myhrer
27	Valerie Stalder
28	Torleif Myhrer
29-30	Valerie Stalder
31	Barber Lines A/S, Oslo, Norway
32-33	Valerie Stalder
34	Osaka Municipal Government
35	Owen Franken
36-38	Valerie Stalder
39	Jack Fields
40	Valerie Stalder
42-44	Torleif Myhrer
45	Valerie Stalder
46	John Gumperz
47-49	Torleif Myhrer
50	Valerie Stalder
51-52	Torleif Myhrer
53	Doris H. Linder
57-62	Valerie Stalder
63	K.K. Breivik
64-66	Torleif Myhrer
67 bottom	John Gumperz
67 top	Torleif Myhrer
69	Chestnut House
70	Valerie Stalder
71-72	Valerie Stalder
73 left	Valerie Stalder
73 right	Torleif Myhrer

All Maps by Donnelley Cartographic Services

Text Acknowledgments

page 54   Dreyers Forlag: "Ash Lad and the Troll" from *Norwegian Folk Tales* by Peter C. Asbjörnsen and Jörgen Moe. Copyright 1960 by Dreyers Forlag. Reprinted by permission.